For Such A Time As This

By

Elizabeth Byrne

For Such A Time As This

By

Elizabeth Byrne

For Such a Time as This

By Elizabeth Byrne

British Library Cataloguing-in-Publication Data

A catalogue record for this book is available from the British Library

ISBN: 978-1-904592-51-8

The Cover is from an original painting called 'Barleyfield'. It is an egg tempera painting by Fergus A Ryan. The view southwards from his house 'Narnia' towards the mountains leads onwards to west Wicklow, and the beautiful road to County Carlow.
The field to the right contains the foundations of a mediaeval farming village associated with St Mary's Abbey in Dublin.
Fergus is leader of Trinity Church Network in Dublin which is linked with Hacketstown Christian Centre.

First Published & Printed 2008 by **Barratt Ministries Publications**
114 Daisy Bank Road, Victoria Park, Manchester M14 5QH, UK.
E-mail: info@barrattministries.org.uk
Web: www.barrattministries.org.uk

Contents

Foreward	9
Introduction	11
1. My Story ...The Beginning	13
2. My Story... God Speaks	21
3. My Story... My Dream	25
4. My Story... We Wanted More	29
5. My Story... New Beginnings	35
6. My Story... God Continues to Speak	45
7. My Story... God and the New Building	51
8. My Story... The Grand Opening	55
9. My Story... The Ghana Connection	59
10. My Story... Their Stories	65
11. My Story... Alan's Story	79
12. My Story...The Potato Seed	85
13. My Story... For Such a Time as This!	91
14. My Story... Why are we Here?	99

Dedication

This book is dedicated to my family, my husband Michael, my sons Alan & Niall, my daughters Aoife and Claire who have supported me throughout my adventures and my beautiful adorable grandson Dylan Lee who has brought such joy to our lives.

Yet who knows whether you have come to the kingdom for such a time as this.
Esther 4v14

This is the day the Lord has made;We will rejoice and be glad in it.
Psalm118v24

Acknowledgements

I want to thank,

God for the breath, life and the many, many blessings that He daily pours out into my life.

My sisters, Sheila, Ann, Margaret, brother Patrick, sister-in-law Ann and all the members of Hacketstown Christian Centre, for always being there for me.

Debbie, Mark, Colm and Rosemary, for loving my sons and daughters.

Breda Rose, Kingsley & Cathy Armstrong for their help in the process of editing this book, and also for their encouragement for me to "step out of the boat" and write it in the first place.

Fergus Ryan for permitting me to use his painting, Barleyfield, from his private collection for the wrap-around cover.

Anna O'Rourke for the personal photograph used on the back cover.

The local Pastors in Carlow and Dublin, Pastors and friends from all across Ireland, UK, Brazil, Ghana, Ivory Coast, and the US.

Foreword

by Kingsley Armstrong

In 1998, I visited Co. Carlow in the South of Ireland and met up with a most interesting group of ladies. I had been travelling extensively and had met many groups in other places, but was amazed by the excitement and enthusiasm of these women. They had been meeting in their prayer centre in Carlow and were captivated by the Word of God

I had honestly never seen anything quite like it. These Christians were so hungry for the Word that they spent hours studying it every day. It was a real joy to build relationships with these wonderful people and to see that friendship grow over the next ten years.

Elizabeth came, initially, with one of my teams to Ghana and caught the 'missions bug'. It is safe to say that she has not been the same since and has returned there many times as well as flying off to other countries.

I have been so blessed by Hacketstown Christian Centre. They have been faithful to me over the years and have been an amazing blessing to the nation of Ghana.

Foreword

I had been saying to Elizabeth that she needed to write a book about her story and how the Fellowship came into being. It is a story of the amazing grace of God, of trust and faithfulness, both on God's and the people's part. Elizabeth has been so faithful to the call of God and God has honoured that.

This book is called, 'For such a time as this'; it records the intimacy of God; His search for the individual; His patience and kindness and His call into the heart of mankind.

This story shows how God wants to put His hand on all our lives and use us in this hour and in this time.
It relates how God takes the ordinary person, the humble, the weak and accomplishes miracles through their hands.

This will inspire you and challenge you. I hope you finish it and say, "If God can use Elizabeth, then He can sure use me!" I hope it encourages you to step out of the boat and dream big dreams for God.

You can do it also; this is your time; this is your day. You can know Jesus today. He loves you; He died for you. Ask him into your heart today and I promise you that you will never be the same again.

It has been such a privilege to introduce this book and recommend it to you. Be blessed as you read and give all the glory to God; God bless you!

Introduction

On the second of March 2008 my beautiful, adorable grandson Dylan presented me with a book called "Grandmother Remembers" by Helen Exley. It's a book for a grandmother to fill in for her grandchild with photographs, letters, personal thoughts and bits of family history. As I filled in the pages and reflected back over my life, I realised how precious life is and that I could have come along at any time but God chose me 'for such a time as this'...

Sections about my Grandparents drew plenty of blank spaces. As I thought about my parents and my grandparents, thanksgiving welled up in my heart to my Heavenly Father for the gift of families ... thanking Him that my children are a heritage from Him and that my children's children, are the crown of their grandparents.

This book is written to encourage you, the reader, to know and believe what God can do with ordinary people, people who live everyday lives doing everyday things and while we have received much from our families our true identity comes from who we are in Him. Our past may have been messed up, mixed up or even too painful to want to remember but when Jesus comes into our lives He makes all things new. He uses me in many ways; He will use you too if you allow Him. He loves you with an everlasting love and He is constant in His affections for you.

Dream the impossible dream. An American President once said "When your memories outweigh your dreams you have now grown old". I intend to continue dreaming new dreams until The Lord calls me home. I intend to go to where He calls me to go, to do what He calls me to do and when I stand before Him, to hear Him say "Well done good and faithful servant...". I intend to finish strong, whilst knowing I can only do this by His grace and strength.

Chapter 1
My Story ...The Beginning

*Before I formed you in the womb I knew
you, before you were born
I set you apart...*
Jeremiah 1 v 5

Life began for me on October the sixth, 1959, in Coolmanagh, Hacketstown. I made my entrance into the world early that morning. I was the fifth child to be born to my parents, and somewhat of a 'surprise', as they had felt that their family was complete after my brother, Patrick, was born.

When my mother had given birth to three daughters, the desire of my grandfather's heart was to see a grandson! So when my brother, Patrick, arrived safely, my parents felt it was 'mission accomplished'.

Well, while my parents had their plans, God had other plans and His plans are supreme, usually very different to ours. My father was 56 years old and my mother was 44 years old when I arrived on the scene. Because my mother was unwell after my birth, my sister Margaret had to take time off school to take care of me.

All through my childhood, God's hand was upon my life, although I did not know it at the time. However, in retrospect, I can see it, having heard about the times when I fell into the fire, ran out in front of a car, of how the pram I was sitting in went hurtling down some steps, toppling over at the bottom, and tipping me out, but still I survived. Why? In hindsight, I believe that God chose me and kept me 'for such a time as this'!

I remember that, as a child, I had many fears in my life. I worried a lot about my parents; my concerns were, I suppose, what would happen to me if they died? Who would take care of me?

I could never come up with any answers to those questions.

My sisters had already moved away from home at this time and the only mode of transport available to my parents was the humble bicycle, so even the 15 mile journey to Carlow town was quite a big thing.

Of all the worries and fears that troubled my young mind, the greatest of all was the fear of death. I thought a good deal about death, wondering if I died was that the end for me, or was there really life after death. And what about hell, was it for real?

My father came from a large family, and many of his twelve siblings emigrated from Ireland, mainly to live in America. Some of his sisters became nuns and continued to live in America, teaching and nursing. Every three years, they were allowed to come back to Ireland on a visit. When they came here, it always seemed as though they were trying to recruit relatives to join their Order and to go back to the States with them.

Some of my cousins did make the move and, as I was the youngest of all the cousins, I felt that there was quite a lot of pressure put on me to plan ahead and think about going there.

In those days, the nuns wore very heavy habits and head gear and all I could see was their eyes. They were also inclined to hug me a lot which I found rather scary. My parents and relatives were not the 'huggy' type, so when these nuns launched their hugs on me I found it a bit disturbing, to say the least! I do not know whether I found the habits or the hugs to be the most off-putting, but they were certainly not going to recruit me!

However, I clearly remember my mother asking them to put my mind at ease regarding my fears of death and hell. She wanted them to reassure me that I did not have to worry about going to hell forever when I died. Looking up at them, at what I could see of their faces, I waited for the answer.

"Oh, Elizabeth, you don't need to worry, dear. You won't go to Hell, because Hell is only for people who commit very bad sins, mortal sins, like murder, etc. You are a good girl, and Honey, if you do all the right things, you will be going to Purgatory, and so you'll be all right, now."

These words did nothing to ease my anguish. To me, purgatory was the same as hell; maybe it did not last quite as long, but there was really no difference.

From that time on, I felt estranged from my family, like an outsider. I just could not share their beliefs or feel comfortable with their religion or their religious convictions. Yes, I believed in God, but always felt as though I was struggling to perform. I tried so hard, over and over, to be 'good'. It was very frustrating! If I did something which I knew to be wrong, I felt so guilty and condemned, powerlessly wondering how many 'black marks' God would allow in His record of all my wrongs before he would finish with me completely.

This was the torment that filled my life; there was no end to it, no way out.

In my teens I believed that I could not feel any love for my father and this was another weight, heaped on my heart, which was already troubled and heavy.

My mother often quoted an old adage, 'You may be able to fool everyone else, you know, but you cannot fool God'.

So during my monthly visits to confession I would confess my sin, do my penance and walk out into the daylight, which always seemed a lot brighter after spending time in the dark confessional. I always felt lighter after getting my sins off my chest and also knowing that I was free for another month before facing the dark room again...

Then one day I accompanied some friends on a retreat, where I found, to my horror, that we were expected to attend "open confessions". My tummy felt ill at the thought of it as this was something completely new to me.

One by one my friends went in, they seemed to be in there for ages and came out looking happy and relaxed, so I thought that either they did not confess all their sins or else they had all been very, very good!

Well, my turn came and as I entered the room I saw a lovely smiling young priest sitting in a chair waiting for me. He greeted me, introduced himself (all new to me) and continued to smile. I took a deep breath and began to pour out my sin of not being able to love my father. Even though I had confessed it before, it still troubled me because things had not changed.

It was not that we were fighting, or that my father had ill-treated me in any way. I had huge respect for this man, who had never laid a finger on me. It was just that with the large age gap, I could not relate to him, we had nothing going for us. If my father had been cruel to me, I would have had a reason, maybe, to feel the way I did; but because he was a good, kindly man it somehow made me feel worse.

Anyway, when I finished my story, I was expecting a tough penance but instead this young man began to share with me his own struggles with his father and how recently things had begun to change for the better between them.

After he had shared *his* experiences, I felt that a huge burden had rolled away from me. I no longer felt guilty and condemned. In fact I came out of there like a calf let loose from its stall!

I did not know, at that time, that God's Word in the Bible tells us 'that we are to confess our sins one to another and pray for one another' (James 5 v 16) and that is what happened for me that day. Never before, when I had gone to confession had someone shared their weaknesses with me!

In those days I went to confession in fear and trembling, but I believe that, through these events, God was preparing me for my walk with Him, which was about to begin. I thank God for the way He used my experiences to strengthen me.

When I committed sin at this time my conscience would tell me that I had done wrong, but later when I got saved through faith in Jesus Christ, the Holy Spirit of God would convict me of my sin and convince me of my need to repent to the Father and turn to Him for forgiveness.

God's Word *says*

> *"If we walk in the light, as He is in the light, we have fellowship with one another, and the blood of Jesus, his Son, purifies us from all sin."*
> **(1 John 1 v 7) and**

> *"If we confess our sins, he is faithful and just and will forgive us our sins and purify us from all unrighteousness."*
> **(1 John 1 v 9)**

> *"He himself bore our sins in his body on the tree, so that we might die to sins and live for righteousness…"*
> **(I Peter 2 v 24)**

Jesus, the divine Son of God, who knew no sin, became sin for us; every sin that you or I could or would commit was dealt with by Jesus at Calvary. We do not have to do penance for our sins, because Jesus paid the price and what a costly price that was. So, when we mess up (as we do), we confess our sin to our heavenly Father. He forgives us because His Son has already purchased our freedom when He chose to give His life for us on the Cross. What wonderful Good News this truth is!

Of course this does not mean that we have a licence to do as we please but yet, when we do miss the mark, big time, or in small ways, we can come back to God through the Blood of Jesus. Our Saviour, Christ Jesus has 'made the way' for us.

For all have sinned and fall short of the glory of God
Romans 3 v 23

There is no sin too big to separate us from God. Sin is sin and Jesus took care of all the sin of mankind when He won the victory over sin and death at the cross at Calvary.

For the wages of sin is death, but the gift of God is eternal life in Christ Jesus our Lord.
Romans 6 v 23

Chapter 2

My Story... God speaks

As life continued on, I finished school and began work, at quite a tender age.

My first job was working as a telephonist in the local post office on the manual telephone exchange and later I worked as a receptionist in a nearby missionary society. While I worked on the telephone exchange, something happened that impacted my life. I believe that God's hand was in this, so therefore, I feel it is important and definitely worthy of mention here.

Back in those days there were very few recorded messages on phones so whenever a telephone operator came across one, we enjoyed passing it on. So down the lines and through the grapevine it went!

One number that I made connection with belonged to a Christian Telephone Ministry in the Dublin area. It was a three minute recording of a passage of scripture from The Bible.

One of the other telephonists connected me to this recording as a joke, just a gag, a bit of fun, but for me, those words were life-changing. They brought me life and peace. Now, I began to feel that maybe, just maybe, I could find the answers to some of my life-long dilemmas in God's Book, the Bible.

I had been brought up to believe that ordinary people, like myself, were not supposed to have access to this Book; it would be too difficult to understand and, anyway, you had to be "special" to even touch one. In fact, I understand that, in times gone by, even the nuns, in their Convent homes were not even encouraged or allowed to have full access to the Word of God for themselves.

At the end of the message, the recorded voice encouraged the listener to get hold of a New Testament and, if this was not easy, well, you could get one by leaving your name and address after the beeps....which I did!

A few days later my New Testament arrived. I was overjoyed, feeling like I had gained something precious, which I had been looking for and that had previously been missing during my life up until then.

Well, the fact of the matter is, without going into much detail, my New Testament was confiscated, so I was back where I started ...or was I?

No, hang on.., I could still dial up that Christian Telephone Ministry in Dublin and listen to the recording. There was still, available to me, three minutes of God speaking to me; always His personal message to me.

I now knew that there was more to God than religion; I realised that God was a God who wanted to have relationship with His people, whom He had created.

He was not a lump of stone, or a block of wood, but a God who was interested in me and desired that I should get to know him better. I began to look out for books and magazines that contained the Word of God, but they were few and far between in Ireland at this time. Yet every little bit which I came across gave me a hunger for more. Some people say that hungry people will eat anything and sometimes that is true but I believe that verse in the Gospel:

> *"Blessed are those who hunger and thirst for righteousness, for they will be filled."*
> **(Matthew 5 v 6)**

I believe that, when we seek God with a sincere heart, then He will reveal Himself to us, by whatever channels He wishes. God can choose to use anyone or anything to reach us. It never ceases to amaze me how God has worked and continues to work things out in our lives. He is so wonderful, so truly magnificent, and yet, our God, the Creator of the Universe, has so much time for us; He loves our company. He wants us, His people, to relate to Him in a special way. Awesome!

Chapter 3
My Story... My Dream

All throughout my life, I had a dream; it certainly was not to go to America (remember the in-family recruiters!) and, no, it was not to have lots of money and travel the world and, believe me, it was most definitely *not* to do a parachute jump!

My dream was to marry at a young age, and have lots and lots of children. The reason that I wanted to get married really young was so that my children would not have to worry about their parents being old, whilst they (the children) were still very young. In this way, I envisaged, my children could never suffer the fears and worries which were part of my every-day life.

When I was 15 years old I met Michael. His family lived close by but he was living and working in Dublin. We became friends and every weekend, when he came home, he would call and visit me. My mother was not too happy with the situation, as she felt I was far too young for him. But in time the family accepted our friendship and later our engagement; this was a joyful occasion which took place on my 18th birthday.

We were married when I was 20 and Michael was 27. This was actually my first time to live away from home. Michael had changed jobs by then and was working and living in Kildare, looking after show-jumping horses. Our new home was about one hour by car from my original home. So, with plenty of mixed feelings, I settled into married life.

This was a lonely time for me as I missed my parents, nieces and nephews, my job, my old work mates and all that was familiar to me. It was a complete new start in a place where I knew no one. I applied for lots of different jobs, but a few months later, just when a suitable position was offered to me, I discovered I was pregnant. I was over the moon!

My son, Alan was born in March 1981. This was one of the happiest times of my life. Now, I felt so fulfilled, as my dream began to unfold. Alan was so cute, so lovely, so much part of my dream come true!

That same year, I had a miscarriage. Sadly, our second baby did not make it into this world. And, so, was the roller-coaster of life, soaring one minute, dipping the next. But overall life was good, but busy!

Before the end of October 1985, I had also given birth to Aoife, Niall and Claire, all beautiful babies, who made my heart do summersaults every time I looked at them. Now, I was 26 years old, married to a wonderful man, with four gorgeous little treasures; so within five years I had achieved all of my hearts' desire.

Yet, there was still a void in my life, a part of my being which did not feel fulfilled. No matter how many children I had to fill our home and keep me a busy mum, there was something missing. Somehow, I kept sensing that there should be more.

A year or so later, we built a house back home, and returned to live quite near the place I was reared and I thought my happiness would be complete. Yes, things were good, but the emptiness was still there. Why?

Chapter 4

My Story...
We Wanted More

Soon after my children were born, both my parents passed away. My father died in August 1987 and my mother in December 1989.

As I sat during my father's funeral service and listened to the words that were being spoken, I was numb. I simply felt removed, cut off, at a distance from what was being said; in fact, from the whole ceremony.

Later, as I tried to explain to my mother how I felt, her reply was "If your father could hear you now, he would turn in his grave".

Regarding religious matters, during my early years, I had felt isolated and different to my family, but now, however, I felt that I must be totally rebellious! I was a complete 'outsider' who could not relate to the tradition in which I was reared. It seemed like I was rejecting everything which I was brought up to believe in.

I did not know where I belonged; actually, I did not seem to fit in anywhere. The old fears of death and hell returned, worse than ever. Now I had even more torment, because I did not know how to talk to my children about God. How could I teach them what I, myself, did not understand?

It was at this time that I became what I can only describe as, a 'walking ball of fear'. I was paralysed by fear. Fear of the unknown, fear of what might happen, fear of what might not happen, fear of God because I felt that I was rejecting His religion, fear of fear; not to mention the old ones, fear of death and hell!

When my mother passed away, I just did not listen to what was being said at the funeral ceremony. Yet something caught my attention. The choir sang a hymn and the words brought a sense of calmness to my heart...

> Be not afraid, I go before you always,
> come, follow me, and I will give you rest.

That was when I spoke to God, "God, if you are really real, please show me how to follow You, and I will follow You, all the days of my life".

Just then a sense of peace came over me, like I had never experienced before. From that day onwards, instead of trying to recite 'prayers', I began to talk to God, just like I would talk to my best friend. I told Him everything, I laughed and I cried; cried like I never had before.

Life changed for me then, in some ways; I felt more determined to find Him. One thing was that I began to pursue a new hobby, which was mountain climbing. I guess I felt that if I climbed the highest mountains, giddy heights, that maybe I would get closer to God! Well, the exercise was great, and I did have fun, and yes, of course I appreciated God's handiwork; the views were awesome, but I still felt that there should be more.

At week-ends I would take my children to the beach, make sand-castles in the soft sand, then run across the hard, rippled sand on our way down to the sea. Splashing in the waves as the tide came in; watching as the waves came to shore, breaking and rushing in, but never crossing their borderline. Yes, I could recognise God in His creation; this had to be God, it was so wonderful! So I continued to talk to Him, but I still wanted to find out more about how to follow Him, and in rural Ireland at that time, there were not many answers.

Then, one day, my eldest sister called me, and very excitedly, began to explain to me about how she had become a 'Christian' and wanted to tell me all about how she now had a wonderful relationship with Jesus. I listened, in disbelief, as she waffled on about how wonderful this new relationship was, etc., etc. According to her, everyone needed to have what she now had! I began to get worried about her; it seemed to me, she had lost her marbles altogether!

Okay, for the past while, I had been 'talking' to God, but here she is, telling me that Jesus is her special friend!

Now, how weird is that? She was even saying His name without lowering her head in a respectful manner. In those days, not one person, from a Catholic back-ground, would ever even mention the name of Jesus without bowing their head and the nearer their head nodded towards their knees, the holier that person was, or so it seemed!

So, here was my sister, with her jargon of "Thank you, Jesus" and "Praise you Jesus" and not even a beck of her head in respect. Now, I was the one saying, "If Daddy and Mammy could see you now, they'd be turning over in their graves!"

Over the next couple of months, I enjoyed teasing my sister, but I suppose I was also debating with her more seriously than I actually realised. I often tried to trap her with awkward questions, but she would always suggest I go find the real answers for myself in the Bible, or as she called it, the 'Word of God'.

My opinion was that she did not know the answers, so she was just fobbing me off, but I did not have them either, so really, I did not have much to lose.

In the meantime, a friend, Anne, whom I had kept in contact with since we had worked together years earlier in the Missionary Society, had also been asking herself questions and seeking answers.
Anne was married now and also had four children, so we had lots in common. When we visited each other, we chatted about our hopes and dreams, our thoughts

and our fears, as our children played together on the floor.

Well, of course, I just had to tell her about my sister and this new freaky faith thing that she had found. I must confess that, sometimes, I added in little bits just to make the stories even funnier.

This became a habit, a part of our conversation almost every time we met, but I noticed, as time went on, that if I was not mentioning my sister's newfound faith thing, Anne would make a point of asking me about her. Later Anne told me that these stories stirred something within her. Deep down both of us knew that we wanted more. I think we both realised that we wanted a personal relationship with Jesus, a relationship that was different from what we both understood to be 'religion'.

You see, religious tradition had not given us any answers and both of us recognised that we had a deeper need, so we decided to see where we could go about finding a Bible study. Yes, this was getting serious now, because we had a hunger and thirst that needed to be satiated.

One day, in Carlow, Anne saw a notice, announcing that a preacher from Northern Ireland was coming to a College there, to share the Word of God. We knew that this was for us and made arrangements to attend that meeting.

Chapter 5
My Story... New Beginnings

He has delivered us from the power of darkness and conveyed us into the kingdom of the Son of His love
Colossians 1 v13

During the week leading up to that Wednesday night meeting, I found that I was having a lot of mixed feelings. I wondered how I should tell Michael, my husband. He was a devout Catholic and took great pride in us rearing our children in 'the faith'. As it turned out, he did not stand in my way.

I was also very excited, although I was not sure what to expect. Somehow, I sensed that something special was about to happen; a new beginning; a new chapter of my life was about to begin.

That mellow August evening in 1992, I set off and met up with Anne along the way. We were in good form and it was great that there were two of us; we made sure that we would get there early so we could get seats in the back row.

But there was rather a shock awaiting us! Never in my wildest dreams did I expect that this was the same meeting as my sister attended. But early as we were, we did not make it there before my dear sister! Yes, there was Sheila, sitting right up the front. I have to admit that it was a bad start because I never meant to attend the same fellowship which she belonged to. Actually, I still felt she was a little bit cuckoo, so the embarrassment of finding myself in the same room was bad enough. But there was worse to come!

The speaker whom we had come to hear was not due to arrive until the following week. In our excitement we had got the date wrong, and had arrived one week too early.

So, guess who was scheduled to speak that night? Yes, it was our Sheila!

She read a Bible passage from 1 Corinthians, chapter 13. I recognised it because it was one of the readings we had used for our wedding. It is all about the love of God. Everything about this prayer meeting was different to anything I had experienced previously. There were lots of strange songs about Jesus, the Name of Jesus and the Blood of Jesus, but there was something about the words of those songs which made me feel good and confident that it was okay to be there. There was life in those songs. I also felt that the people here were truly worshiping God, not just singing songs.

After Sheila went through the passage from the Bible, she invited all of us to 'share' what we got out of it. I was amazed at how many people spoke out what it meant to them. I never thought so many people could get so much from a scripture passage. Another thing we were not used to was people saying stuff like 'Amen', 'Alleluia' or 'Praise the Lord' during or after her reading. We also heard 'Thank you, Jesus' which was even stranger. So I was thinking, "I won't be getting too deeply involved here". I was pretty sure that I would never want to find myself speaking like those people.

At the end of the meeting, everyone was invited to come forward if they had prayer requests or needed prayer for healing in any area. Well, they lined up, and my goodness, I could hardly believe my ears! The things that they were asking God for were just amazing. Not only that, but it was apparent that they actually believed that God would hear and answer their prayers. Many were thanking Him for the favourable answers in advance of receiving them!

Anne and I tagged onto the end of the queue and finally it was our turn. Some of the leaders prayed with both of us individually and we both chose to say a prayer, inviting Jesus into our lives, to be our Lord and Saviour. Neither of us had any hesitation; we didn't need time to think about it, but, as we later realised, some other folk do need to take a lot more time with a decision like this. In hindsight, we both felt that it was because we both had been seeking Him, so deeply, each in our own way, for so long, and this was the reason that the Lord speeded up the experience for us. Some other friends, who joined us (and Him) later, took a lot longer with those life changing decisions, but they also had to meet with the Lord at the point of their need, before they could jump over the fence.

This whole experience was completely new to us, but I believe God had prepared us both, in advance, for this night. We were both hungry and thirsty for the things of Him. We were desperate to receive a personal touch from Him. So, as we trusted in Him, the Lord showed us that He was ready and willing to receive us, just as we were.

We were elated; there was nothing to compare with this. As I drove the car home that night, it just felt like the car had sprouted wings, and was flying through the air. I had never before felt so free or so in love. I thought, up until then, that the love I had for my family was the greatest and highest form of love, but now this brand new love I felt for God was causing my heart to race, and praise and thanksgiving to my Saviour was flowing from my mouth at a pace I did not even know I had. God had given me a new language and I just babbled away to Him.

The fear, which my life had been full of, was the first thing to be broken. From the moment I accepted Jesus into my life, as my Lord and Saviour, those fears just dispersed. They melted, like snow in sunshine!

Michael was the first person to notice. He realised that I was a happier and more relaxed person and that I no longer insisted that the back door was locked all the time. Sometimes, when he came home from work, he would find me singing at the top of my voice, lost in praise and worship. My new relationship with Jesus was wonderful and beautiful and the freshness of it made me want everyone else to have it too! Then, I understood that my sister Sheila, was not cuckoo; she was deeply in love with the Lord Jesus, and out of that relationship, she felt compelled to tell other people. Yes, at last, I got it, because it was exactly the same then for me.

I wanted to shout it from the mountaintops. In those early days, I told everyone I met about this new relationship I had found with Jesus and people did not understand how a quiet and timid person like myself suddenly had so much to say. Normally I was never loud or talkative.

Anne and I continued to travel over to Carlow every Wednesday night to the Prayer Meetings and we also went to other Bible Studies and Conference Meetings. In fact we went to as many as we could possibly attend. Because we were so hungry for the things of God, we felt that we did not want to miss out. While many of our friends at that time would have chosen to curl up on the sofa and follow the 'soaps' or maybe branch out to catch the 'bingo bus', we were spending our quality time at meetings or at home reading through our Bibles, so God could personally teach us from 'His Word'.

From the moment I got my own Bible, I knew I had something very special here. As I read it, I knew my

Heavenly Father was speaking to me, personally. All my questions were answered within this Book.

Anyone who enjoys reading knows that even the mustiest, dustiest book, with yellow pages, can come to life when a person opens the pages and begins to read. But let me tell you, that no book has Life, like God's book, the Bible, has Life. God, the Creator of Life, has Life in His Word and when you open that Book, and ask Him, by His Holy Spirit, to reveal to you what you need to know, please be assured He will do just that! Sometimes, it seemed to me, as though certain verses were almost jumping out of the Bible at me, as God high-lighted the answers to my questions or my prayer requests.

Now, thanks to this Word of God, I knew, that I knew, that I knew, that I had eternal life! I knew that I would never perish and that there was nothing anybody except Jesus could do to get me saved; no person living or dead, no denomination, no good works, nothing and nobody except Jesus!

Jesus Christ, the divine Son of God had purchased my salvation at Calvary.

> *For God so loved the world that he gave his one and only Son, that whoever believes in him shall not perish but have eternal life*
> **John 3v16**

And this everlasting (eternal) life is this, knowing the only true God and knowing Jesus Christ whom He sent.

My prayer life changed, my way of living changed; I had become a new person, the old was gone; the new had come.

Every morning, after I would leave my children to the school bus, I would cycle three miles to work. I always enjoyed cycling but now the three miles were just not long enough. I would sing and praise God all the way and always felt that I got to my destination too quickly. Sometimes the weather would not be so favourable and the wind could be very strong and I would ask the Lord to protect me and I knew He would. I would often pray in my new spirit language, especially if I was unsure what to ask for in prayer, because I now understood that if I prayed directly from my spirit to God's Holy Spirit, I was praying according to His will, not mine.

I continued sharing my experiences with people and many were open to listen and to hear my heart. Some may not have been sure of what this was all about, some may have been plain curious or possibly sceptical, but for whatever reason, they began to accompany me to the prayer meetings in Carlow. I do believe that those people saw a remarkable change in me, which led them to have an interest in what I was up to.

As more and yet more people became interested in Bible study, etc. and continued to travel over to Carlow, I considered hiring a bus, for practical reasons, and also for the encouragement that a group will bring to each other.

However, after prayer and deliberation, I felt that the Lord was showing me another way.

I chatted with Michael, and once I realised he was not uncomfortable with the idea, our first meeting for Hacketstown, Clonmore, was scheduled to take place in our home on the twenty eighth of April 1994.

As the news spread around the local community, I soon realised that interest was increasing and many more people would like to come, apart from the group who were already travelling to Carlow.

Our home was not going to be big enough! So a close neighbour, who was also very enthusiastic, decided to ask the local Priest for permission to use the community building, which was beside the Catholic Church in Hacketstown.

That night, our first prayer meeting took place in St. John's Hall in Hacketstown. The meeting was scheduled for 8.30pm and we had put out a circle of chairs. Soon those were occupied, so another circle was added, and more circles of chairs squeezed in, until the room was full.

There were many local people, but a group from Carlow also came over to offer support, and more importantly, to share from the Word of God and those brothers and sisters in faith, were also available to pray with anyone who needed personal prayer or had prayer requests at the end of the evening.

Yes, I truly believed that this was the beginning of a work of God! But, actually, if I knew then what God was going to do, through me, I would have run a mile away.

Yes, our God amazes me in the way He does things; He just shows us part of His plan, little by little, piece by piece. He had bigger plans for Hacketstown, but as yet, I was blissfully unaware of them.

That night began as a strange, almost scary, first time experience. Yet it was a wonderful night and I was so full of thanksgiving because I believed so many people were truly blessed with the beginnings of a deeper relationship with God. Much later when I got home, I was just feeling more in love with God than ever before. As for me, I now knew that I had found (received) a priceless pearl, the real thing, so nothing less could ever satisfy me again...

> *Love is patient, love is kind. It does not envy, it does not boast, it is not proud. It is not rude, it is not self-seeking, it is not easily angered, it keeps no record of wrongs. Love does not delight in evil but rejoices with the truth. It always protects, always trusts, always hopes, always perseveres. Love never fails.*
> **1 Corinthians 13:4 - 8**

Chapter 6

My Story...
God Continues to Speak

Throughout these early years God truly showed us His favour. He blessed us by bringing Christians from Carlow, Dublin, and all around Ireland, North and South to share His Word with us. Not only that, but powerful support arrived from the UK, America, South America and many other far flung places! When I met those people, even for the first time, it felt like I already knew them. There is always a bond, a sense of oneness, because people who treasure that special relationship with God are like 'family'. It is a wonderful and amazing thing when we can instantly trust complete strangers and invite them into our lives and our homes without hesitation.

When the time came for us to move out of St. John's Hall, we were allowed to use a room in the National School. Later, I was blessed to be able to open up my home to the group, as we felt the need to have a more structured Bible Study on Tuesday nights. Soon, my living room was not able to house the ever growing bunch, so we got permission to meet in the Church of Ireland Hall in Slate Row for Tuesday night studies and our Sunday Services. I firmly believe that God's hand was in all of this and that he softened hearts of people to accommodate us.

You see, although we were blessed, and we knew it, in these days in rural Ireland, we were also misunderstood. Some people were quite annoyed with us, some were fearful that there was a weird 'cult' in their midst and others just thought we were raving lunatics!

For our part; well, we loved the Lord Jesus more than we minded being misunderstood, so we just continued on. Nothing anyone could say or do would stop us.

Easy for me to say, but it was not always so easy for my children! From time to time they got it tough, as they had to listen to their school mates making fun of me. Still I believe God always protected them and in time they learned to trust Jesus and the power of their prayers.

One day my son came home from school, threw down his bag on the floor, looked at me and said,

"That`s it! Tomorrow, I will burst him"

"Burst who?" I asked.

"John Brown" (not real name)

I said, "Darling, Christians don`t fight!"

"Well, you don`t know the names that he has been calling you, and it has gone on too long now, so tomorrow I'm gonna burst him"

Sensing his frustration, all I could do was reach out with the Word of the Lord,

"God`s word tell us to bless those who curse us, to do good to those who hate us and to pray for those who spitefully use us or persecute us".

Together, we prayed a short prayer for this young man and over the next few days, I continued to declare, according to God's Word, that 'no weapon formed against my family would prosper, in Jesus name'.

A week later, choosing a relaxed moment over dinner, I enquired of my son how things were now with him and 'John', and he told me that everything was fine; in fact, it was as though that incident the previous week had never happened! There is power in prayer, there is power in God`s Word and God gives us the grace and strength to overcome everything that comes against us. This is just one of many happenings which I could write about, but it is the one that springs to mind now as I write.

We then had regular meetings on a couple of week nights, as well as on Sunday mornings. Several mornings or afternoons also, smaller groups of us would meet to pray together for our families, our communities, our needs etc. In our twos and threes, we got together in each other's homes or in our cars if the homes were too busy. Some of the group went 'prayer-walking' together, availing of a bit of exercise whilst joining together in prayer.

> *Again, I tell you that if two of you on earth agree about anything you ask for, it will be done for you by my Father in heaven. For where two or three come together in my name, there am I with them."*
> **Matthew 18:19-21**

I continued to travel over to Carlow, usually a couple of nights each week. Looking back now, I do not know how I managed to keep abreast of all that was going on in my life. I worked outside the home, looked after my family and still managed to give Michael a hand on the farm when needed. God definitely blessed me with good health and energy and I was filled with zeal; ready to go that extra mile. Life was hectic, in a good sense, by no means trouble or problem free, but generally good.

The Christian life is exciting and wonderful, but of course, it is not a bed of roses. It is not always easy to be different; certainly it would be easier to run as part of the crowd. I loved the people here in my community. Right here, in the neighbourhood where I was born and reared, and had married into a local family also. My family roots were in this area. However, tradition was very much part of rural Ireland. Sometimes, if one broke out of the traditional mould, that person was deemed to be different and maybe at times I felt that I just did not fit in.

Ours was also, and still is, a close-knit community. The folk here do support each other, especially at times of need. In the event of a tragedy or misfortune, people would always rally round and lend a hand, glad to be able to do something useful, to assist in any way.

That is still the case today and I thank God for this nation, and I continue to pray to God to visit us in a powerful way; yes, every city, every town, every village, every hamlet, every townland and crossroads in the nation. I believe every man, woman and child was created for relationship with the Creator. Jesus desires a personal and intimate relationship with you and me. That special relationship will change your life, just as it changed mine!

So often people believe that if they do and say all the 'right' things, it will make everything OK and proper with God, but nothing, only a relationship through Jesus Christ will work. Seriously, I tried all avenues and only bound myself up, more and more. If there had been another way, believe me, I would have found it, because it was not for lack of searching! Now, I realise that my searching was groping in the dark, because at that time I had not encountered 'The Light' of the world!

> *In him (Jesus) was life, and that life was the light of men. The light shines in the darkness, but the darkness has not understood it.*
> **John 1 v 4, 5**

Throughout these early years of 'knowing' God, He spoke to me through His Word, like I never knew was possible. In the world that we live in, there are many voices, but God has told us in His Word that "His sheep hear His voice and they know Him".

Before my personal encounter with Jesus, I had prayed for years, but was never sure if God even heard me, let alone really cared about me, but now I was communicating with God Almighty by the power of His Holy Spirit, and He was giving me the grace to live a Godly life in these times. Even saying it, to myself, as I write, it is an awesome thing! How great to know that God the Father, Creator of Heaven and Earth, loves each and everyone of us so very much!

Knowing Him, trusting and serving Him, is the best way of life for any and every man, woman and child on the planet. He is our Shepherd and promises to be with us every step of the way.

Chapter 7

My Story...
God and the New Building

As time moved on, our love for God just grew more and more; our relationship with Jesus became stronger and stronger. Our prayers were always in line with God's Word. We loved to study our Bibles, and even though we were still misunderstood by many, we found that the Christian walk was the best ever.

In January 1997, I felt that the Lord was speaking to me, during my prayer times about having a building, a place of our own, to meet and fellowship in.

Yes, of course, we appreciated the hospitality we had received locally with the halls that we were renting. But to have our own place would be fantastic, and as I felt that this would take a long, long time to happen, I gladly said "Yes, Lord, let's go for it".

I suppose, my thoughts were, at the time, that this would surely take many, many years to achieve, as our budget was limited (to say the least), and finding the right site would probably take ages. Really, I guess, I was thinking that by the time it would come to pass, I would be out of the picture and someone else would have the responsibility of doing this work.

Well, that is not the way God works! His ways are not our ways, and His thoughts are not like ours. One chilly morning, in November 1998, as I was dropping my children off at the school, I noticed a sign in a garden close by, which stated "Sites for sale, apply within".

Wow! My tummy started to do summersaults and I felt a real excitement in my spirit. I was not sure why, but I knew that this was from God! The next day, I found myself knocking on the gentleman's door, making enquiries about the site for sale. He actually had two sites for sale and was willing to give me the choice as to which one we would prefer.

This was to be the start of a wonderful, exciting, and frightening adventure!

We had not a clue what to do next, but little by little, bit by bit, person by person, God showed us and taught us. We prayed about everything and sought the Lord's will in everything. To this day, if someone asked me the question, "How did it all come about?", I simply cannot answer them! It simply could not have happened without the 'gift of faith' and God's intervention!

First the site, then the building; everywhere we went, we experienced God's favour! We had favour with the building society, the solicitor, the people in the county council offices, the builder, everyone that was to help with the planning and building of our new place!

We watched in amazement, as, like pieces of a jig saw puzzle, everything fell into place. So many people were used of God to make this happen, and to all these people, we are truly grateful.

For fear of leaving anyone out, I have decided to mention as few as possible by name.

While, on one side we were being blessed and enjoying the favour of the Lord, simultaneously we were experiencing some opposition from other areas.

I am also very thankful for the struggles etc., that we went through, even though at the time it was very painful. But because of it God was able to develop the character of Jesus more in our lives. It is easy when things are going our way but when they are not we need to press in more to God and receive of His unfailing love for us. When times are tough we just have to depend on Him more and more, to spend more time with Him and bask in His Presence.

Whenever we move forward in life there is a price to pay. The Promised Land may flow with milk and honey and there may be an abundance of fruit in the land but most of the time, we find that the giants live there, too. Giants of fear, rejection, jealousy, negativity, suspicion, criticism, disappointments, and opposition are some of the ones we come up against when we step out of the boat.

In March 1999, we signed and paid for the site. At this point we had received the full planning permission necessary to start building. So, then it was full steam ahead...

On a cool, fresh spring morning in May, filled with excitement and apprehension, we stood back and watched the digger go on site to commence the work.

Over the next number of months the work continued and by October 1999 we were ready to celebrate our Opening Night of Hacketstown Christian Centre!

Chapter 8
My Story...
The Grand Opening

For now I have chosen and sanctified this house, that My name may be there forever; and My eyes and My heart will be there perpetually.
2 Chronicles 7:16

God is Spirit, and those who worship Him must worship in spirit and truth."
John 4:24

October the seventh 1999. The great day had dawned and we were fast running out of time. Someone once said that God is never too early or never late, but that His timing is perfect!

What a day it turned out to be, hectic, to say the least! We waited for our last stage payment to come through, so that we could pay the builder and collect the keys.

The electricity was not yet connected, but again, we experienced favour, this time, thanks to a kindly neighbour, who allowed us to connect into his supply for the night!

As we put the finishing touches to the main rooms, the carpenter was fitting the kitchen which was finally complete at 8pm, just as the celebration was about to begin. Yes, it was a hectic day, but very special; one that will live with me forever.

As so many things were being done at the last minute, it seemed that God was throwing in lifelines to meet our deadlines.

We were joined by people from north, south, east and west of Ireland, people from the community, local leaders and pastors. The atmosphere was exciting as the room quickly filled up to overflowing.

The main speaker at our celebration was a Brazilian pastor who had lent us support at that time. Jean-Carlo Aché, his wife Flavia and family were living in Carlow town for a season and working with the local churches.

It was a very special night; we sang, prayed, had tea – it was 3 am before I left; it was indeed a wonderful night and God was glorified!

Later, we received sound teaching from Jean-Carlo, and interestingly, it was he who introduced us to 'The Headway Discipleship Series', three little books of short day-by-day readings which cover an immense amount of practical topics for the Christian life. Fergus Ryan is the author of those books, and this encounter much later led to our affiliation with Trinity Church Network in Dublin of which he is the Senior Leader.

Chapter 9

My Story...
The Ghana Connection

During 1997 - 1998, The Lord had brought a Course our way, which was called 'The Joshua Project', signed, sealed and delivered by a gentleman, named Kingsley Armstrong. This young man, Irish by birth, was living in Wales and was president of IGO, (International Gospel Outreach).

It was an incredibly, wonderful course! We were inspired and encouraged to recognise the potential inside each and every one of us, to dream the impossible and believe in our dreams; not only that, but to learn to laugh at impossibilities and discouragements, I could go on and on...

We were motivated to be brave and fearless and keep our eyes fixed on Jesus, to take Godly risks and step out of the boat, to walk on water, just as Jesus (and Peter) did! The Joshua Project encouraged us to move onwards and upwards, not to waste our time dwelling on past mistakes or wallowing in self pity because of criticism, which mainly came from the 'dry boat sitters' anyway. This course was a tremendous encouragement to us during our 'building season', as we learned to encourage ourselves and ignore and overcome negativity.

Our work in Africa began in 1998 when we heard that IGO were raising funds to send to Ghana, to supply a long awaited and much needed bus to a very poor area, in the centre of the capital city, Accra.

Kingsley had already been to Ghana and IGO were supporting a work there, named 'Rescue Aid Mission', headed up by Pastor Osmond Owusu. Our contribution reached IGO just after they had reached their target for this particular assignment and the funds were already transferred. However, we were assured by IGO that there were many other needy projects under the auspices of the good Pastor Osmond, so they would direct our gift towards the 'Orphans and New Orphanage Fund'.

Kingsley became one of the brothers who stayed in touch, visited fairly regularly, and always brought life and spiritual encouragement, not to mention the bit of fun and a few good laughs!

A born Evangelist and Missionary, he continued to visit Ghana every year and, in time, many other countries besides. During a week-end with us, towards the end of 2004, he asked if I would consider joining with a team he was leading to Ghana in January 2005. Again, although the thought excited me, I timidly thought, just like with the building of the Centre, this would be a dream come true, but not likely to happen for quite a few years yet.

That evening at home, snug before the fire, I broached the subject with Michael, really expecting him to put me off the idea. Well, what a surprise awaited me; far from being negative, Michael actually encouraged me to grasp this opportunity that was presenting itself! He said, sure, if I wanted to travel, why put it off? He was quite prepared to take care of the family and look after things on the domestic front.

So, I speedily booked my ticket, applied for the visa, got all the necessary jabs and away with me! This was the first of many visits to Ghana and what can I say, I fell completely, head over heels, in love with this country and its people.

On the final Sunday of that first wonderful mission trip, I was privileged to be one of just two people from that team, who were brought to visit a tiny, remote and very poor village.

From the first mention of going to Africa, it had been my desire to experience part of the village life. The sprawling, hectic, busy city life, teeming with people was certainly a new adventure. Some were probably rich (by comparison), and many more, yes most of them were really poor, they were all in your face, desperately trying to sell something to eke out a living, but deep in my heart, I knew that I wanted to get to the desolate areas, spend time there and see for myself how the country folk lived! Maybe, it was because I am from a rural background, that I felt the urge to identify with those people. As it was my first time to visit, and I was conscious that I was 'part of a team', I just did not feel it was my call to speak out and say what I wanted to do, or where I wanted or go to; after all there was a programme already in place. The preferred choice, for me, was just to go with the flow, and that's was what I did, trusting God, but of course, He knew my heart, and I was so thrilled with this opportunity.

Well, that wee village really did catch my heart, Now, I knew for sure that if there was going to be a work in Africa, for our part of the Church body, it would definitely be focussed on the villages.

Thus, from humble beginnings, began this special, on-going relationship between Hacketstown Christian Centre and Rescue Aid Mission.

Our next project was to send a 40ft hi-cube container load of aid to Accra. With surplus money left from sending the container, we were in a position to purchase some land on our next trip in Jan 2006.

From July 2006, I began taking teams from our church, the locality and just about anyone who heard about this mission and wanted to join in! Like me, those who came caught the passion and the vision for this work and were and still are a tremendous blessing and encouragement to me.
A school was built; wells were drilled, as time went on, we felt the need to have a separate fund (bank account)

for all the work in Africa. This was named VIP – (*Villages In Progress*).

Rathûil International School is no ordinary school! Since it opened in October 2007, Pastor Richard has been inundated with people who want their children to be enrolled! Numbers doubled between 2007 and 2008 and there is a long waiting list! Why? Because this school has the standard of excellence; Richard has been mightily blessed with a Godly vision and standard, way beyond what he sees before his eyes.

VIP now supports the parents – children who cannot afford fees (the majority) by way of a sponsorship programme; we pay modest salaries to the teachers, maintenance and upkeep of the school and of course the children are fed at the school and medical supplies are available to them. The VIP fund has also been used to assist with the completion of the Home of Hope Orphanage, and we sponsor orphans and destitute children there too. Aid has been delivered to the pupils at the School for the Blind in Akropong and Jamestown School in a tough area of Accra has received assistance occasionally. From time to time, under the leading of the Lord we have supported individuals, perhaps paying college tuition fees, the gift of a lap-top computer or setting them up in business, with a sewing machine or some tools.

More than anything, we respect and appreciate the desire of the African people to learn; school is hugely important to them. They love to better themselves and they dream big dreams. It is a privilege to work with them and see some of those dreams materialise.

Chapter 10

My Story... Their Stories

In this chapter I want to move from 'my story' to 'their stories'. Everyone in the Fellowship has a wonderful story to tell and several wanted to include their story in this book. Each is recorded in their own words....

Margaret McGrath

I was born and reared in Coolmanagh, Hacketstown, where I married and settled, right next to the house where I grew up.

My parents were hard-working, religious people. To me, God was someone distant, someone way out there and yet I had a hunger and thirst to get to know Him in a real way.

About 16 years ago, my youngest sister, Elizabeth, brought me to a Christian meeting. It was wonderful; everyone there was so full of joy and I could see the peace on all of their faces. That evening, I invited Jesus into my life, to be my Lord and Saviour.

> *That if you confess with your mouth, "Jesus is Lord," and believe in your heart that God raised him from the dead, you will be saved.*
> **Romans 10:9**

My life completely changed after I put my trust in Jesus. I am so happy and feel so blessed in every way; I can now manage anything. With Jesus in your life, nothing is impossible. Having a real relationship with Him is so amazing, and I can do things I never imagined I could do, because He has enabled me to do them. I can get up every morning, knowing that I am not alone. I have an excitement about life. The big thing for me is that I can involve Him in everything I do and then I can handle anything that comes my way.

I know that He knows exactly how I feel every day and where he is taking me and there is great security for me in that!

Before I got close to Jesus there were many dark days in my life, as I suffered from depression. Often I thought that I would never see the light at the end of the tunnel. But God brought complete healing, wholeness and restoration into all of my situations.

> *In him was life, and that life was the light of men. The light shines in the darkness, but the darkness has not understood it.*
> **John 1: 4,5**

Life is an adventure and the world is my oyster now.

With my new-found confidence, I was able to go to Ghana, where I had a marvellous time, painting the school and playing with the children. It was wonderful being able to be a part of the teams bringing love to many. As the song says, I can walk tall and straight and look the world right in the eye.

God gave me great strength when my husband, Pat underwent surgery and had a major bypass. I also had a hip replacement before I went to Ghana for the first time.

Although I do not always get things right, He will not abandon me when I get it wrong. He is always there to help me along the way. As Jesus is now the Lord of my life, knowing Him and His love for me is amazing.

By asking Jesus, God's son, to be the biggest part of your life, you will discover the very purpose for which He created you.

There is nothing and no one else who can do this for you. Jesus said,

> *"I am the way and the truth and the life. No one comes to the Father except through me."*
> **John 14:6**

> *"Salvation is found in no one else, for there is no other name under heaven given to men by which we must be saved."*
> **Acts 4:12**

God loves you and has a wonderful plan and purpose for your life, too. He wants you to call on Him, so He can share every moment of your life!

Breda Rose

Before I went to Ghana in January 2006, someone said to me, "When you come back, you may decide to write about the experience of your first ever mission trip, so use your five senses to take in everything".

And that's exactly what I did!

After chilly temperatures in airports at Dublin, Teeside and Amsterdam, I knew we had 'arrived' when we stepped out of the plane into 28 degrees heat in Accra, the capital of Ghana and home to 2.5 million people.

The night-time ride through the streets –at times, no more than dirt-tracks-was my first experience of Ghana.

Although simple, there was a liveliness about the streets. I was soon to realise that this sprawling city, teeming with people, never sleeps; the continuous honking of horns became part of the back-ground noise, day and night-time alike!

Arriving at our hotel, which might seem basic by European standards, we were quick to note that it boasted every necessary requirement in each room, a refrigerator, stocked with bottled water (supplied by our host), noisy air-conditioning and a shower with an ample supply of cold water. (The veterans on the team, who had made this trip many times in the past remembered when none of these 'luxuries' were standard).

On walk-about the first morning after arrival, the thing I was most conscious of was the sight and smell of the open sewers, set in concrete trenches on each side of the street, the senses were working all right! Not something I would have expected to find in a city but it is surprising how quickly one adapts; after a few days I was stepping over them as I crossed the road with hardly a downward glance.

What I never got used to, though, was the sight of all the things that women and men alike carried on their heads. My nieces who have visited New York tell me that it is hard not to keep looking up at the tall buildings, skyscrapers, but for me in Ghana, it was hard not to stare at all the wares which were being transported head high. Huge flat dishes or plates, piled high with fruit, sometimes sliced, sacks of potatoes, basins of live fowl, shopping bags, stacks of cardboard boxes and huge plastic packs, containing cartons of drinking water were commonplace, with the vendors weaving through three rows of traffic, attempting to sell their wares through car and minibus windows.

Another popular street-selling commodity is a plaintain crisp, made from a variety of banana, which is sliced very thinly and resembles our potato crisp.

But the most amazing sight had to be a young woman carrying a lighted fire in a steel basin across a city open park area while she sought a spot to put it down and cook for her family. We could only assume that the basin must have been two-tier, with water underneath or surely otherwise her head would have burned!

Of my visit, the biggest impact was most definitely, the children. I absolutely fell in love with each and every one, despite being warned by an English pastor who was part of the team, that they were little thieves, inclined to steal one's heart! The warmth, the love that emanated from each one of them, the interest in white people, with not the slightest bit of antagonism; if we carried sweets, they eagerly accepted and appreciated these gifts, yet if we didn't have goodies, they were equally receptive of us, just loving to be asked their name and to shake our hands, over and over again.

The thing that shocked me most was the absolute number of children. I find it difficult to express in words the large number of children everywhere we went, many, many more than I could have expected to see.

Each individual face was so beautiful, so expectant. On leaving the crèche area of one orphanage a little guy, maybe 18 months old, maybe older, dashed out and grabbed me by the leg. As I looked into that little face, while peeling him off my leg, all I could think was, "This one, if only I could even bring even this one child home with me".

But there was an extra-special highlight for the Irish team. Elizabeth had decided prior to this visit that she would buy some land on which to build a school, so

Osmond took us to meet the village 'chief' so the deal could be arranged. Despite how strange it seemed to us, this was the correct and legal way to proceed in an African village. I was privileged to be in attendance as Elizabeth was taken to the chief's home.

The chief, whom we addressed as 'Nana' sold us the land for a reasonable price, as he was pleased that a school (which would also serve as a church) would be built there.

As Elizabeth was the initiator of the arrangement, she earned herself the title of "nkoso hemaa" (pronounced 'kowso heman'). As part of this ceremony, before being seated in the chief's chair, she was dressed in royal robes and jewellery (which unfortunately) she was not permitted to keep. Our British friends like to call her Queen Elizabeth III, as a result of this event. Even as I sat there I could hardly believe it was real. I did not even realise I was perched on the edge of my armchair until Elizabeth whispered, under her breath, that I should sit back and relax.

Our visit passed all too quickly, but having caught the vision, life will never be the same for me again. When I got home, I thought it was irrelevant whether I go back in the near future or not, because part of me will always be there anyway. But now three years later, I am getting itchy feet as I would love to see the progress for firsthand, for myself.

I really love to see new people on every team which goes out because I feel so strongly that one has to see it for themselves; visiting the country with your five senses alert, and an open mind and heart are what it takes. Every person needs to create and live their own experience, you cannot build on someone else's. Before I went, Elizabeth had shared her experiences from the previous year with all of us, but it just does not impact you in the same way as your own experience. Most of what she told us, I only remembered when I was actually there, seeing, hearing, feeling, tasting, and smelling for myself.

To close, I would like to express my grateful thanks to Elizabeth; in appreciation for all that she has done and continues to do for all of us in Hacketstown Christian Centre. I know I can speak for all of those who have included testimonies in this book and also those who have not!

Elizabeth is a true leader and a true friend to all of us! I am also thankful and grateful to her wonderful family, who have released her to do the Godly work she does 'for such a time as this'.

Anne Kirwan

Jesus said, I am the way, the truth and the life, no-one can come to the Father except through me.
John 14:6

In May 1992 my father passed away and at that I time I was thinking about my life and the future. I had four children, a husband and a home to look after, and was quite busy with this, but often I would look out the window as I washed the dishes and think about life and death.

OK, I was happy, I loved my husband and my children, but still I felt that there was something missing. I did not know what it was, but I knew it had something to do with God. I remember buying a book entitled 'The Happiest People on Earth' and as I read it, I realised that these people had a wonderful relationship with God and I wanted to find out more.

I chatted about all those things with Elizabeth, who was a good friend, and also seeking God in a new way, so, together, we were on a journey. We discovered that there was a prayer meeting in Carlow, which might fulfil our needs, and we decided to go along.

On that cool August evening in 1992, a life-changing decision awaited me! That night I asked Jesus Christ to come into my heart and into my life. This decision has changed my life forever and I know that I will go to Heaven when I die, because I understand that Jesus died (and rose again) for me and all mankind on that cross at Calvary, two thousand years ago! All of my sin is forgiven and I can have an audience with God at any time. He is interested in every area and detail of my life; my joys and sorrows, and he loves me, unconditionally.

The next day, I knew I was different, but just could not describe it to anyone; it was something I felt within myself! No, of course, all my troubles and cares did not disappear at once, but I had a peace on the inside of me that I had never experienced before in my life.

During the last sixteen years God has brought me through many trials and difficulties. In 2003, I faced the biggest trial of my life so far, the death of my 18 year old son, Paul. It was a dull, cold Saturday in December when Paul left home to go play a soccer match. He played soccer most Saturdays so this was not unusual. Late in the evening, we got a phone call from the team manager to say that Paul had been injured and was being brought to the Doctor. He was then sent to Beaumont Hospital in Dublin. I thank God we had two days with him; to talk and pray with him. The last words he spoke to me were, "I love you, Ma". His condition worsened over the next seven days and on 29th December 2003 he passed away.

Six weeks before Paul passed away, he asked Jesus Christ into his heart and his life. This was a re-commitment, because Paul, just like his brother and sisters, had already given his life to Jesus. But as this was so recent, it gave us great peace and encouragement, after his death, to know that he was in Heaven and that one day I will meet him again. All through the nine days when Paul was in hospital, that peace never left me, even though my heart was breaking, for my son.

It was like as though God had his arms around me, and has kept them around me ever since then.

> *But I do not want you to ignorant, brothers, concerning those who have fallen asleep (died) lest*

you sorrow as others who have no hope. For if we believe that Jesus died and rose again, even so God will bring with Him those who sleep in Jesus.
1 Thessalonians 4:13-14

For I am convinced that neither death nor life, neither angels nor demons, neither the present nor the future, nor any powers, neither height nor depth, nor anything else in all creation, will be able to separate us from the love of God that is in Christ Jesus our Lord.
Romans 8: 38, 39

Ann Howard

As a child I had a dream that someday I would go to Africa and help the poor people there. Maybe I could become a nurse when I grew up and then I could go? Anyway, the years passed, I married a wonderful man called Anthony. In time we had two children, Shane and Laura and life was good.

HCC became involved with another wonderful man, an African, named Osmond. As we became aware of the needs in Ghana, the work began. We rolled up our sleeves, so to speak, and organised a container load of goods to go to Accra, the capital.

Fundraising began also, and Anthony did a parachute jump. It was great to be involved; as we knew that all the money was going directly to Osmond, who would use it to assist the people most in need. Schools were badly needed, as the poor people could not afford to send their children to school. Elizabeth decided that

HCC, with God's help, could provide a school and a plot of land was purchased.

In 2006, Elizabeth asked if anyone would like to go to Ghana in July to view the progress that had been made. I immediately said 'yes' and waited for my dream to become a reality. I was so excited and all the plans were made for me to go. My best friend, Breda Murphy, was coming also so that was an extra bonus!

Then a few weeks before the trip, I became very ill and ended up in hospital. The doctors could not find out what was wrong. I was extremely weak but during all of this time I prayed and asked God for healing. I remember one day when Elizabeth phoned I was so weak I could hardly speak but I was aware that she and all the members of HCC were praying for me also. I knew that God's plans and purposes for me were to go to Ghana and deep in my heart I knew it would come to pass.

Philippians 4 v 13 tells us that we can do all things through Christ who strengthens us, and that is exactly what happened for me. I recovered in time to make my first trip to Ghana in July 2006 and I had an absolutely wonderful time, blessed to be 'healthy' and strong while I was there! I thank God for making it all possible.

I returned to Ghana in March 2008 and was doubly blessed when I saw when I saw how much more progress there was in those couple of years. The school, which also serves as a church building was built, the orphanage complete and wells bored for fresh drinking water in the villages. Most importantly we have wonderful friends there now.

Dream big dreams; never give up because with God, all things are possible. I could have listened to all the negative words, saying I was far too sick to travel to Africa, but we need to stand firm and trust in God and we will be greatly blessed.

> *But thanks be to God, who always leads us in triumphal procession in Christ and through us spreads everywhere the fragrance of the knowledge of him.*
> **2 Corinthians 2:14**

Finally, in this chapter, a poem from Renate

NOT LIFE'S PAWN BUT GOD'S POETRY

My life is a poem written by God with great passion
saturated with His love is every thought and line
like the designers of high fashion
He is committed to beauty, detail and uniqueness
for that life of mine

Often I don't co-operate and slow the process
work out my own moves, play my own game
then I go running to God with my loss
flinging myself into His arms for restoration
again and again

So my life-poem includes many verses
that have turned out to be quite rough
it is because they are written in my own hand
and not by my Father and His love

I decide to place the pen back into His hand
and let Him continue writing my life-story
my trusting in His loving guidance
even brings Him Honour and Glory

What a privilege to be part of the great story
of this world wide family of His
and knowing that He is right now with me
"For such a time as this"

Chapter 11
My Story... Alan's Story

> My Son, Alan, has written this chapter to be included in the book. It gives a different perspective from one inside my family!

A son's perspective, of a mother, a person and a grandmother!

As a 'Mammy'

My first recollection of organised 'religion' was the early Sunday morning trips to 8am Mass in the Church in Hacketstown. All of us kids were loaded up in the car and told that if we were good all throughout Mass, we would be allowed to get a '10p mix-up' (sweets always went down well, of course!) from the little shop across the road from the Church. At that time, Mass and everything associated with it was completely over our heads, because all I can remember was that we sat in the same seat every week, which was the row with the pillar in the middle of it. We, as children, did not know any different; we were brought up as Catholics, we went to Catholic schools, so as far as we were concerned, Mass, Priests and Church life, as we saw it, was all there was; it was the norm.

So when a group of women started to meet in our house in Clonmore, on a Tuesday night, with their Bibles in hand, you could not really blame us for feeling a little bit uncomfortable with this new and strange situation, but we did find some humour in the unfamiliar words and noises that were coming from the front sitting room. To our ignorance we later found out that they were actually speaking 'in tongues'!

But as time passed and the meetings continued, we probably relaxed a bit more, while we were around it all, without fully understanding what was going on. The trips to Mass decreased, while we were encouraged to go to 'meetings' in Carlow a lot more. I vaguely remember these meetings, but do recall feeling a little uncomfortable attending them, as I did not like participating too much. I do not know if it was because it was all new to me or because I am a quiet person, who likes to keep my thoughts, feelings and beliefs to myself, but I do remember feeling a little bit envious of some of these people who could express themselves so openly and publicly.

As time passed, Mammy became more and more involved, and you could easily see the change in her! Life did not seem to be such a struggle anymore; she could draw strength from her new way of life and was always encouraging us to do the same for our lives.

As a mother, Mammy has given us the best upbringing which she and Daddy could have done; we never wanted for anything that we needed; we were taught to work hard and respect others. As the eldest I probably felt that I was treated the hardest, but I can understand that, all the more now as I am a parent myself! I can actually see myself being hard on my son, even though Dylan is still very young. Why? Because I want the best for him, and I want him to be the best that he can be!

As a parent we cannot fault mammy, we are very proud of her and all I wish for her now is to slow down a little bit more and enjoy her life to the full and, of course, enjoy her grandchildren.

At this time, I was big into the athletics; I was lucky enough to be good at it, so there was probably a competition on most weekends. Before every trip that we went on we had to 'get prayer'; although most times I probably resisted. I did know she really believed what she was saying; it was not just like the 'bless yourself with the holy water' which I feel is done more out of habit than belief, it was something bigger than that, not just a tradition and I really knew that!

I can remember the time when Mammy got it into her head that she wanted to build the Christian Centre. We at home surely thought that it was just a phase she was going through, and that it would pass, but as it turned out, this is now a fine building that all associated with can be very proud of, and take great pride and pleasure from.

Hacketstown, like most rural towns in Ireland with a big Catholic influence, would be very set in its ways, so to have something like a Christian Centre built on its door step might not go down well, but that never discouraged or disheartened Mammy!

Although I probably do not know half the things she went through at that time, my biggest fear was that she would be jeered and mocked as such. I can remember the time that she told us where she had decided that The Centre should be built, and that it was going to be right beside the school we attended! Needless to say that there were a few unhappy people in our house around that time; they were more worried about what their friends would be saying than anything else. I can honestly say that it did not bother me too much where they decided to build.

Actually, I would like to think that if I shared one thing in common with my mother that it is strength of mind, and belief in my own decisions, free from outside influences, let that be peer pressure or whatever.

It is now around ten years since Hacketstown Christian Centre came into being and at this stage I would like to think that Mammy knows we have done, and will continue to support her, both in past exploits and future dreams. Although at times, it may seem as if I do not approve of things that she does, or sets out to do, but yet this is out of protection, rather than lack of support for her. I would not like to think that people would take advantage of her good will and gain from it.

The Centre in Hacketstown and all the people who go there, are an inspiration to others on the 'outside'.

Whether it is a family tragedy, or a personal obstacle, they can draw such unbelievable strength from their belief in such trying times. It is at times like this, that one can see just how deep their belief goes, and it is encouraging to know that one can draw such strength from it. I am envious that I do not or cannot show the passion that they can!

As a person

As a person, Elizabeth is probably the most inspirational person I know. It is sad that I should wait to write a piece for a book to tell her so, as I do not have to go any further than home to find a real hero, who has gone completely against the grain; in a very religious community; taken everything that has been thrown at her and kept on turning the other cheek, knowing that she was going to come through, on the other side, with the victory that she always dreamt of and knew was there. My mother, Elizabeth, is a constant rock for so many people who depend and rely on her for support and advice; the type of person that everyone should aspire to become.

As a Gran

As a grandmother now, she is patient and kind and most of all, extremely generous with her time! She has been there for us, Debbie and I, on many and numerous occasions, especially when we have been under pressure, and I am truly grateful to have her as the grandmother of our son, Dylan.

Elizabeth is very special, and for everything that I have said, my brother and sisters would ask me to include them as being in total agreement!

Chapter 12
My Story...The Potato Seed

As a child, and growing up in a rural area, there were some events that would seem special, even if you hated them! Sowing the potato seeds was one of those for me. It was an annual event and also a ritual! My father spent a long time preparing everything for this time. The ground had to be ploughed, drills made, manure added and then the seed potato was carefully sown. The seed sowing was my job!

To ensure that I was accurate in my work, my father would give me a length of stick to measure the correct distance between each potato seed. Ploughing and drilling was done by horses pulling the plough; the rest was manual work. I always understood that although those 'seeds' were leaving my hand; they were not leaving my life. Soon the lush green plants would grow, white flowers appear and then die back and then we would be back, digging out and picking an abundant crop from beneath each potato stalk where an individual seed had been sown.

As a teenager, I helped a local farmer as he sowed potato seed with a tractor and potato sower. I would sit on the potato sower, count one two and drop and watch as the sower would do its work covering the seed as we went along. I was always happy to do this job, as I would get a little pocket money and also I knew that I would not be called upon to pick these potatoes, so I could relax.

As a grown-up, and married to Michael, I continued to sow potatoes; even when the children came along, and they helped also. Sometimes, as I would sit on the seat of the potato sower, I would cheat a little, counting one, two, three, four, five and drop! I guess I knew there would always be enough. As sure as the seasons come and go, I would be back in that field, picking a copious harvest, enough potatoes to last our family for many months,

So from the time I was a little girl and throughout my life, the humble spud has taught me a very important lesson in sowing and reaping...

> *Remember this: Whoever sows sparingly will also reap sparingly, and whoever sows generously will also reap generously. Each man should give what he has decided in his heart to give, not reluctantly or under compulsion, for God loves a cheerful giver. And God is able to make all grace abound to you, so that in all things at all times, having all that you need, you will abound in every good work.*
> *As it is written: "He has scattered abroad his gifts to the poor; his righteousness endures forever."[1] Now he who supplies seed to the sower*

> *and bread for food will also supply and increase your store of seed and will enlarge the harvest of your righteousness.*
> **2 Corinthians 9:6-10**

I learned that no matter what seed leaves my hand, yet it never leaves my life. As committed Christians, we as a group have seen time and again, that no matter what we sow into God's kingdom, especially in the area of finances, those seeds return a harvest, more than we could ever expect. God has prospered us individually and prospered us as a Church. We have seen our children blessed, as our families have experienced the goodness and favour of God.

We live in what has been called 'The Upside-down Kingdom' meaning that God's ways are not man's ways of doing things! The natural order of things would say that if you give, then you won't have, but God's order of things is quite the reverse. His Word says;

> *Give, and it will be given to you. A good measure, pressed down, shaken together and running over, will be poured into your lap. For with the measure you use, it will be measured to you."*
> **Luke 6 v 38**

In the Bible during times of famine, God prospered his people, so no matter what recession comes our way, the people who put their trust in God don't have to live in fear and dread of lack.

So many times in my life, especially when I go to Ghana, I am amazed at how the money stretches. I stand in awe of the work which has been done and think, "God, This is You at work! You are truly amazing"...

The Principle of the Seed

Then God said,"Let the land produce vegetation: seed-bearing plants and trees on the land that bear fruit with seed in it, according to their various kinds."And it was so.
The land produced vegetation: plants bearing seed according to their kinds and trees bearing fruit with seed in it according to their kinds. And God saw that it was good.
Genesis 1 v 11-12

Each one of us is predestined to be conformed to the image of Christ. The law of the harvest is "everything after its kind." If you plant corn, corn will grow. The life of any organism is in the seed, and all the possibilities of that life are there. It is truly amazing. The entire colour, beauty, symmetry, is in the life. For example, take a look at a rose. No one has to paint or perfume it. All that you see, the colours, the perfect petals, the fragrance you smell, came from the life in that tiny seed. The principle of the seed is true for all forms of life; plants, animals, human beings or spiritual beings. Peter wrote about spiritual beings.

"Being born again not of corruptible seed, but of incorruptible, by the word of God, which lives and abides forever".
1Peter 1v23

Paul said, "That seed was Christ".

**As believers we are reborn of the seed of Christ. It's like being born a second time. This is the reason that Christians are called 'born again believers'. For example, on 6th of October, 1959, I was born to my parents, Elizabeth & Patrick Byrne, Coolmanagh, Hacketstown. In August 1992, when I committed my life to Jesus Christ and personally asked Him into my life, as my Lord and Saviour, I was reborn (born again), as a child of God. This is a personal decision every person must make, having reached an age to reason this for themselves.

In 1959, I was born into a sin-damaged, corrupt world. The first Adam had opened a door to sin, so I was a 'natural sinner' from the moment of my birth.

But Jesus, the second Adam, turned things around for us; when He gave His life for us on the cross. As the spotless, blameless, sinless One, He made a way to the Father, for each and every one of us... who give our lives to Him! That is the 'Good News'!

So, at age 33 years, when I invited Jesus into my life, I had access to the Father, in and through what Jesus had done, and all by the power of the Holy Spirit.

Actually, at that moment in time, I was transformed and sanctified! This was not about 'me' doing anything great, but all about simply accepting what Jesus had done for me (and every other person on planet earth). In fact, I became a saint! Yes, seriously, the definition of a saint is 'holy, set apart from evil, sanctified'.

So there are really no 'special' people who attain this title.

Paul, yes, Paul was a saint, but he called all the believers 'saints'. Every Christian believer is a saint! Peter was a saint, but not because of any great works he did, but just like Mother Teresa, he was a saint because he entrusted his life to Christ!

So, when we say things like this, and sometimes they are difficult for people to accept, we are not boasting or thinking that we are something special. The truth is that the Special One is in us. Jesus, our Lord and Saviour, lives within us, because we personally invited Him into our hearts and into our lives. He is the Righteous One and our righteousness is in Him alone.

I am aware of my 'true identity' now because my identity is in Him, the Lord Jesus Christ.

** extracts from the Headway Discipleship Series used with permission of the author

Chapter 13

My Story...
For Such a Time as This!

LÁ LEITHEID SEO AMA

When I was just a little girl
I asked my mother, what will I be
Will I be pretty, will I be rich
Here's what she said to me.

Que Sera, Sera,
Whatever will be, will be
The future's not ours, to see
Que Sera, Sera
What will be, will be...

Those were the lines of an old Doris Day song my mother used to sing at home.

It may have sounded quaint, but it is just not true. Life is not meant to be just a case of hit or miss, come day, go day, wishing it was some other day.

God has a plan and purpose for all our lives; he is a relational God and he wants to be involved with us.

This is a wonderful day to be on planet Earth. The average number of days in an individual's lifetime is 25,550 days. But we do not know for sure if we will see tomorrow! No matter what age any of us are, we could be near to the end of the time allotted to us. Just as a day came for us to be born, so there will come a day for us to die. Between birth and death, God reveals the plans and purposes He has for us, through His Word and by His Holy Spirit.

In the book of Esther we read about a young and lovely Jewish girl who showed tremendous courage in difficult times. She was an orphan, and her uncle, Mordecai looked out for her.

Because the King's wife, Vashti, had publicly disobeyed him, Esther had the opportunity to become his wife, a royal and noble queen. So the king had unknowingly married a Jew. Queen Esther was very precious to him. In chapter 2v7 we are told that Esther was lovely in form and beautiful in features. She was a chosen one. But Esther's new position really came about because God's hand was upon her life, not because of her ability, beauty or anything else. God's hand is also upon my life, and yours, for such a time as this.

The Jewish nation was facing a huge crisis. An evil man named Haman, who had influence with the King, had commanded that the Jews be destroyed, annihilated, completely wiped out. They were doomed to die, every man, woman and child, 127 provinces in all. This was all done out of jealousy and hatred of Mordecai. Haman also had plans to have Mordecai hanged; in fact he built high gallows especially for this purpose.

Mordecai, who had raised Esther after her parents died, sent a message to her, asking her to use her influence with the king to save their people. Esther had great respect for Mordecai and had always been obedient to his wishes.

However, what he was asking of her now was a huge thing. You see, going in to see the king, without being summoned, was not allowed. The law dictated that such an action might very well be met with sudden and violent death.

Mordecai speaking:

> *"For if you remain silent at this time, relief and deliverance for the Jews will arise from another place, but you and your father's family will perish. And who knows but that you have come to royal position for such a time as this?"*
> Then Esther sent this reply to Mordecai: *"Go, gather together all the Jews who are in Susa, and fast for me. Do not eat or drink for three days, night or day. I and my maids will fast as you do. When this is done, I will go to the king, even though it is against the law. And if I perish, I perish."*
> **Esther 4 v 14 -16**

By contrast, how different it is for us, who can boldly and confidently enter into the presence of the King of Kings, our Lord of Lords, and have the assurance that He will always welcome us in His Throne-room, and he delights in answering the requests we make in our prayers of faith.

Esther had not been called before the king for thirty days, which made her task even more difficult. It would have been a lot easier for her to forget that she was a Jew and that she was the only one who could help her people.

She could have just continued to live the 'high life' without endangering her royal and comfortable position with the king. But, Esther trusted in God and cared for her brethren, and in humility she called for a period of prayer and fasting, in which she also joined, in unity with her fellow countrymen and women. Esther also used tremendous wisdom when she did approach the king to ask him to countermand a decision which he had already sanctioned. I believe this was Godly wisdom, received as a direct result of that season of prayer and fasting.

Whereas, Esther was facing a proud, perhaps even an arrogant king, with her requests, we bring ours to our Father, our God of love and mercy.

And yes, Esther did find favour with King Xerxes. The situation was completely reversed; Mordecai was honoured, the Jews were saved, Esther retained her position and the evil man, Haman, reaped what he had sown.

I believe in the power of prayer and fasting, not because we are in terror of putting our requests before our God, but because when we deny our flesh, we can come before the Lord in humility. We also put ourselves in a more spiritual position to hear from Him. There are times to pray and times to listen, for that quiet still voice as He speaks into our hearts.

And I can honestly say that God has turned around so many situations in my life, which I believe to be as a direct result of prayer and fasting. It is one of the most powerful instruments that we have as Christians. It works, but even if it did not, and if I could not think of any other reason to engage in it, I would always say that I want to do it simply because Jesus Himself did. He also encouraged his disciples to pray and fast when faced with difficult situations and in need of serious prayers answers!

> *This is the day the Lord has made; we will rejoice and be glad in it.*
> **Psalm 118v24**

Life is a gift! Before I get out of bed in the morning, I thank God that I am alive. I begin each and every day with thanksgiving. I am thankful to God for my health, my home, my family, the food I eat, the clothes I wear, the air I breathe, my list is endless. Life is fragile, we will not always be around; so we need to make the most of each and every moment as it happens. Yesterday is history; tomorrow is a mystery, so we really only have 'the now'!

We can waste or we can invest our time!

On the waste road, we can mumble and complain about things, but all the mumbling, grumbling and complaining in the world will not sort out our problems.

Investing has different results: God desires us to be a thankful people. Seeds of discouragement cannot take root in grateful hearts, so we need to be grateful! I know at times that life can deal us blows. I have had my share too, but no matter what is going on around me, what storms, etc., I can always have God's peace in my heart. God brings me through over and over again. Our problems never come to stay; they come to pass.

The apostle Paul knew what sufferings were, yet in 2 Corinthians he wrote about our 'light afflictions'!

> *Therefore we do not lose heart. Though outwardly we are wasting away, yet inwardly we are being renewed day by day. For our light and momentary troubles are achieving for us an eternal glory that far outweighs them all.*
> **2 Corinthians 4v16-17**

When, like Paul, we view our troubles as light and momentary, we show God that we trust Him in all our situations. We could choose to allow ourselves to stay awake all night worrying, but what good will that do? What can we achieve by worrying or striving? Nothing, because worry is just about the most useless and time-wasting exercise we can indulge in.

We can keep our problems in perspective by seeing them in comparison to the greatness of our God, who has come through for us again and again. Our afflictions are subject to change, and even if we have been praying about something for a long time, God may well be working in the situation behind the scenes, or perhaps, He is waiting for the right time, and when God is involved, His timing is always perfect.

Our afflictions are temporary and they are working for us, perhaps a far more exceeding and eternal weight of glory than we may ever even realise.

Why not use this day to magnify the Lord, more than ever before?

This is the day the Lord has made, no ordinary day, this day is a gift. We are here for such a time as this!

No matter how impossible something looks, it is not a big deal to God.

Our God is able to turn our stumbling blocks into stepping stones. Sometimes we can make big things out of little things, which do not need a big thing to be made out of them!

Of course, some things are big; some things are very painful, like cancer, divorce, rebellious children, etc. I do not want to minimise anything, but God promises us that He has us in the palm of His hand and that He will never leave us or forsake us.

God has brought me through so many times, in so many ways and He does it again and again. What a wonderful time to be alive, we are blessed, we are chosen and we should encourage each other to run the race that God has put before us. No one starts at the finish line, we all have our own race to run, from the starting line, I have mine, you have yours. We are not competing against each other; each one of us will receive our own individual prize, so we can encourage each other along the way. We are all pressing towards the goal, to win the prize which God has awaiting us as He gives us that upward call.

I press on toward the goal to win the prize for which God has called me heavenward in Christ Jesus.
Philippians 3 v 14

Chapter 14

My Story...
Why are we here?

Thank you for reading this book; I hope that you are enjoying it and that it is both a blessing and encouragement to you. I hope that you can see Jesus throughout the pages and that he is speaking to you. It may be that you want him to do the same in your life as he has done in mine. He loves you so much today and desires a relationship with you. Why not start a new chapter in your life? You can use the prayer printed at the end of the chapter.

Why are we here?

The reason we are here is to **bring Jesus to people and people to Jesus.**

We want to see God's kingdom come – which is, that His will would be done on earth – in Hacketstown and the surrounding areas – **just the way it is in heaven.**

It is all to do with Jesus defeating the things that sin has done to hurt people and to prevent them becoming the magnificent human beings God intends.

True Jesus-type Christianity means forgiveness for everything we have done wrong, release from all kinds of captivity, beauty instead of ash-heap lives, healing of brokenness, and a life of true praise to God, instead of the darkness of despair. Jesus' mission is about **transformation**, not just about **information.**

The Gospel of Jesus Christ is the greatest love story ever written!

> Jesus loves me this I know,
> For the Bible tells me so…

Mary and Joseph were far from home because of imperial rule, a peasant mother giving birth in unsanitary, substandard housing conditions. There was no fanfare, no royal delegation! They laid Him in that manger and watched His little face and they listened for His breathing, just like most parents do.

God had waited so patiently for One to be born into our world who was willing to manifest the amazing, outrageous love which God, Father, Son and Holy Spirit has for us. The Highest of all the High Kings came into our world in the lowest of circumstances, He came simply to serve.

> *For God so loved the world that he gave his one and only Son, that whoever believes in him shall not perish but have eternal life.*
> **John 3 v 16**

> *Neither height nor depth, nor anything else in all creation, will be able to separate us from the love of God that is in Christ Jesus our Lord.*
> **Romans 8v39**

What peace the knowledge that God loves us and accepts us brings!

No matter where we live or what condition we find ourselves in.

No matter how far we might stray away or how unfaithful we are,

God the supreme lover will pursue us in love for eternity!

It is a love that never stops shining. Jesus loves you; you are important to Him no matter what has happened in your life.

If you would like to say "Yes" to Jesus just where you are right now, here is a prayer to receive Him into your life as your Saviour and Lord.

> Lord Jesus, I confess that I have been wandering around following my own way and that I have sinned against you.
> I return to You now and ask You to forgive me for my sin.
> I thank You, that You took that guilty place on the cross which should have been mine.
> I receive You now as my Saviour and I submit to

You as my Lord.
Come into my life and baptise me in Your Holy Spirit.
I reject the devil and all his works, and every claim he has on my life.
By the power of Your Spirit, I will follow You in Your kingdom, now and forever.
Thank You for giving me new life and making me a child of God.

Amen.